Beagle
PATROL

Rob Waring, *Series Editor*

T0052114

HEINLE
CENGAGE Learning

Australia • Brazil • Japan • Korea • Mexico • Singapore • Spain • United Kingdom • United States

Words to Know

This story is set in the United States. It takes place in the state of Florida and at international airports around the country.

Florida

Orlando

CANADA

UNITED STATES

Florida

MEXICO

N
W E
S

A **A Dog's Sense of Smell.** Read the paragraph. Then write the correct form of the underlined word or phrase next to each definition.

All dogs have a very good ability to <u>detect</u> smell, but beagles have an especially powerful sense of smell. Experts estimate that they can identify <u>scents</u> from 1,000 to 10,000 times better than humans can. Because of their powerful noses, beagles are often used as '<u>detector dogs</u>.' These dogs <u>sniff</u> suitcases and packages to find out what's inside. They often work at airports to make sure that no illegal <u>imports</u> get into a country.

1. things made in other countries that are brought into a country: _____

2. the smell that is left by a person or thing: _____

3. notice or find: _____

4. breathe in air with the nose; smell: _____

5. dogs which perform the special task of using their noses to find things: _____

B Detector Dog Training. Read the paragraph. Then match each word or phrase with the correct definition.

Before they begin patrolling airports and other places, detector dogs are first trained at the National Detector Dog Training Center. There, canine instructors teach the dogs to smell the seams of suitcases and other bags in order to check for illegal items. These items include certain types of food—particularly fruit—which may carry flies and other pests that can cause diseases. They also include meat products, which can carry the very dangerous hoof-and-mouth disease.

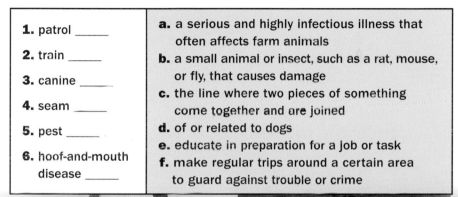

1. patrol _____	**a.** a serious and highly infectious illness that often affects farm animals
2. train _____	**b.** a small animal or insect, such as a rat, mouse, or fly, that causes damage
3. canine _____	**c.** the line where two pieces of something come together and are joined
4. seam _____	**d.** of or related to dogs
5. pest _____	**e.** educate in preparation for a job or task
6. hoof-and-mouth disease _____	**f.** make regular trips around a certain area to guard against trouble or crime

Protecting American Agriculture

For canine instructor Brent Heldt, every day has a noisy start as he stops to say hello to a half dozen or more beagles. When he walks through the dog housing unit at the National Detector Dog Training Center in Orlando, Florida, the dogs bark and jump impatiently. They can't wait for their chance to go outside for a training session and morning run with Heldt.

The first lucky dog is a beagle called Stockton. "Go on, go get it! Go get it!" says Heldt as he throws a ball for the beagle. Stockton runs quickly across the training yard and races back with the ball. However, Stockton wants to have a little fun and he runs right past the waiting Heldt. The trainer laughs as the dog runs around him and keeps the ball away from him. Later he and Stockton will be working hard, but first, it's play time. It's because of these little signs of **personality**[1] that Heldt sincerely enjoys working with the dogs. "Their personalities are all very different," he explains. "That's what makes this job so **cool**.[2] I mean, every time I train these guys, I learn something different."

---

[1]**personality:** the character of a person or thing that is shown by actions, behavior and thought processes
[2]**cool:** *(slang)* fun and interesting

🎧 CD 1, Track 01

Later that day, Heldt puts Stockton in a truck to go to work. No, it's not to go to Heldt's job, it's to go to Stockton's! Stockton is training to become a detector dog so he can work at the international airports around the United States. Detector dogs use their famous noses to sniff for goods which shouldn't come into the country.

Airport detector dogs often wear green jackets to indicate that they are on the job. They then patrol the airport and smell suitcases for foods like **citrus fruits**,[3] mangoes, and apples that may carry fruit flies and other pests. They also sniff for meat products that may carry diseases, such as the dangerous and highly infectious hoof-and-mouth disease. The dogs must learn how to do this without bothering the passengers who are bringing home safe and legal gifts for their friends and family. That's why the dogs must first learn how to 'sniff out,' —or find and signal—illegal imports in the airport baggage claim area. This is where the National Detector Dog Training Center comes in.

---

[3]**citrus fruit:** fruit such as oranges and lemons

At the Training Center the dogs start slowly and simply by first investigating boxes that contain various items. Heldt explains how it works: "What we [have] got here is a target box," he says as he opens one of the boxes. "It's called 'mixed,'" he explains, "The reason I call it 'mixed' is because that's exactly what it is. It's mixed **odor**."[4] He then picks up some of the items in the box and explains what they are, "We have some **beef jerky**[5] [so] I have the beef odor. I have an apple odor. I have [a] citrus odor, and I have [a] mango odor." Stockton begins his training and must first practice finding certain scents like these in a room full of target boxes.

After the boxes, Stockton graduates to working with **carry-ons**[6] and soft-sided bags. He runs around a group of bags with his nose to the ground as he tries to sniff out the target scents. Then, Stockton moves on to the really difficult challenge—finding specific odors in the larger, hard suitcases. Stockton must also learn to behave when he finds a target scent. He must learn to sit down on or near any bag that contains a smell that could possibly be trouble. "That's a good boy," Heldt says to the beagle encouragingly when Stockton finds the meat scent and sits down.

---

[4] **odor:** smell
[5] **beef jerky:** a snack food made from dried meat
[6] **carry-on:** a kind of small bag that one can carry on an airplane

Heldt talks a bit about how the dogs do it. "What we want the dogs to do is [to] work the seam of the suitcase because the odor comes out from the seam," he explains and points to the section where the two sides of the bag join. "What we teach the canine officers and the dogs, [is that] when we breathe the bag," he says, "odor is coming out of the bag." As he talks, Heldt pushes down on a bag so that air comes out the sides to demonstrate the point. By breathing the bag, the canine officers can help the dogs better detect suspicious scents and odors.

As Stockton continues his training with the larger suitcases, he's once again successful. "What have you got? Have you got something Stockton?" asks Heldt when Stockton sits down on the bag. "Good boy! You found it, you found the meat! That's a good boy!"

Things don't always go so smoothly for Stockton though. On the next series of tests, he makes a few errors. He lies down when he is supposed to sit. On another test, he gets too far ahead and pulls away from Heldt until Heldt finally has to remind him, "Where [are] you going? Wait for me!" He then jokingly says to the dog, "You've got to work with me. I'm your partner, remember?" All the while though, Heldt continues to laugh and encourage Stockton. Even though it's serious work, it always has to be fun for the animal.

Scan for Information

Scan pages 15 and 16 to find the information.

1. What are the two main qualities of a good detector dog?

2. What happens to dogs who don't qualify to become detector dogs?

So what does it take to be a detector dog? Heldt explains the qualities that these talented dogs require, "Obviously, number one, they have to be great with people and children, because when we work them in the airports, that's what we're working with—the public coming from foreign countries." He then continues to explain what helps to train a good detector dog, "They've got to have [a] real[ly] good food drive because they work for food." He then adds jokingly, "Anybody who has a beagle knows they love food. Even after they eat a big dinner, they're still ready to eat some more."

The dogs that Heldt trains as detector dogs come from **animal shelters**[7] or are given to the center by people across the country. However, sometimes after the initial training, not all of the dogs are good enough to wear the official green jacket and become detector dogs. So what happens to them?

Heldt explains that they are given to families who want a dog as a pet. "For some reason if they don't work out, we place them in homes," reports Brent. "They stay with us until we can find a home that suits them and we have applicants on our **adoption**[8] list all the time. And we **screen**[9] [the people] to make sure they're also a good fit for the dog that we have."

---

[7]**animal shelter:** a place where unwanted animals live and are cared for
[8]**adoption:** the taking of an animal or child into one's home and taking responsibility for it
[9]**screen:** carefully examine a person to judge if he or she is right for an activity or job

But what about Stockton? How is he doing? Well, his chances of becoming a detector dog look very good. He's progressing faster than some of the other dogs at the training center. He also seems to have the right kind of nature and character since he's a meek, or gentle, dog. Heldt explains why the beagle may be doing so well: "His **demeanor**[10] is really meek, he just **rolls along kind of like a tortoise**."[11]

According to Heldt, Stockton is also good at his job because he's so calm and he likes what he's doing. "Nothing **fazes**[12] him," says Heldt, "He loves working. It's a game to him, which is really important." As Stockton finishes a training exercise in which he has performed particularly well, Heldt picks Stockton up into his arms and continues to encourage him. "Good job! Good job, very good!" he says as he rubs the dog's head and smiles. When the two partners are working together, it's easy to see that it's not only Stockton who loves his work!

---

[10]**demeanor:** manner; way of behaving
[11]**roll along like a tortoise:** *(unusual expression)* is calm and unchanging like the land turtle, noted for its large shell and slow motion
[12]**faze:** disturb, worry

Identify Cause and Effect

Circle the cause and underline the effect in each of the sentences.

1. Detector dogs that aren't good with people can't do the job well.

2. Beagles are given food if they have worked hard.

3. If a beagle can't be a detector dog, it goes to live with a family.

After You Read

1. Stockton and Heldt _____ together before they _____ .
   A. walk, relax
   B. play, train
   C. jump, run
   D. exercise, work

2. What does Heldt explain about the dogs in paragraph 2 on page 4?
   A. They are very serious.
   B. They work too hard.
   C. They are fast runners.
   D. They are individuals.

3. What does the word 'signal' mean in paragraph 2 on page 7?
   A. give
   B. search
   C. indicate
   D. investigate

4. Which of the following is NOT part of Stockton's job?
   A. meeting people
   B. wearing a jacket
   C. smelling fruit
   D. eating meat

5. Why does Heldt call Stockton a 'good boy' in paragraph 2 on page 9?
   A. because Stockton is like a child to him
   B. to show Stockton that he's doing well
   C. to make sure Stockton likes him
   D. to tell others that Stockton is a boy

6. An appropriate heading for page 9 is:
   A. Training from Boxes to Bags
   B. Training Center Rushes Dogs
   C. Animals Eat Fruit and Meat
   D. Stockton Finds Scent and Stands

7. On what part of the suitcase should detector dogs focus?
   A. the side
   B. the carry-on
   C. the top
   D. the seam

8. Which likely describes Heldt's attitude towards Stockton?
   A. nervous
   B. obedient
   C. encouraging
   D. uncomfortable

9. On page 15, the word 'qualities' means:
   A. benefits
   B. characteristics
   C. options
   D. placements

10. What does the writer try to show about beagles on page 15?
    A. People motivate them.
    B. They eat too much.
    C. This work is appropriate for them.
    D. They lose focus easily.

11. In paragraph 1 on page 16, 'them' refers to:
    A. dogs that fail to become detectors
    B. people working at animal shelters
    C. trainers like Brent
    D. Stockton and all other detector dogs

12. What does the writer think will probably happen to Stockton?
    A. He will live with a loving family.
    B. Brent will adopt him.
    C. He will wear a red jacket.
    D. He will succeed at his job.

Springfield's
HEROIC DOGS

The City of Springfield's
Search and Rescue Team Website

A German Shepherd SAR Dog

Training a Search and Rescue (SAR) Dog

Search and Rescue (SAR) dogs are specially trained to find and save missing or injured people, but how is it done? To train SAR dogs, people pretend to be 'lost' so the dogs can 'find' them. Friends of Springfield's SAR Team often find themselves going into the woods and staying there until a trainee dog finds them. As people walk along, up to 10,000 tiny bits of material containing their own particular smell are left behind every minute. SAR dogs can easily detect these bits of scent. The trainer just gives them an item of clothing from the lost person and the dog can simply follow its nose to find the person.

In the five years between 2003 and 2008 the Springfield SAR Team responded to 122 calls for help. Of these 122 calls, SAR dogs were able to help almost 40 percent of the time. Here are a few of our more unusual success stories:

Springfield SAR Team Search and Rescue Statistics 2003–2008

Missing Person Calls	Number of calls received asking for help in finding a missing person	**122**
Direct Finds, Humans (living)	Number of people found directly by the dogs	**24**
Assisted Finds, Humans (living)	Number of people found by people after dogs led searchers to a particular area	**11**
Direct Finds, Humans (not living)	Number of people found directly by the dogs	**9**
Assisted Finds, Humans (not living)	Number of people found by people with the help of dogs	**3**
	Total Finds and Assisted Finds of Humans	**47**

A Surprising Hero

Elementary school teacher Carolyn Rubin has been a trainer with the Springfield SAR Team for four years. She was out for her usual run one sunny Sunday morning in the spring of 2002. Her own SAR dog, Lucy, was with her. As Rubin followed a jogging path into a wooded area, she suddenly realized that a shadowy shape ahead of her was a large black bear—and it was coming directly towards her! Luckily, Lucy immediately started barking and biting the bear's back legs and eventually scared the animal away.

The Right Place at the Right Time

In February 2004, David Roycroft, a local dentist, was skiing alone in Canyon Park. Suddenly Roycroft heard a loud noise. He looked up the hill and saw a three-meter wall of snow heading straight for him. A moment later he was under it. If a person remains under snow for 30 minutes, he or she has only a 50 percent chance of survival. Luckily, Springfield SAR member Jeannie Neal was skiing nearby with her dog, Rusty. Rusty was able to locate Roycroft by his scent and dig him out within ten minutes. This was a first human direct find for Rusty and the dog seemed as happy about it as Roycroft!

CD 1, Track 02

Word Count: 373
Time: _____

Vocabulary List

adoption (16)
animal shelter (16)
beef jerky (9)
canine (3, 4, 11)
carry-on (9)
citrus fruit (7)
cool (4)
demeanor (18)
detect (2, 11)
detector dog (2, 3, 7, 13, 15, 16, 18, 19)
faze (18)
hoof-and-mouth disease (3, 7)
imports (2, 7)
odor (9, 11)
patrol (3, 7)
personality (4)
pest (3, 7)
roll along like a tortoise (18)
scent (2, 9, 11)
screen (16)
seam (3, 11)
sniff (2, 7, 9)
train (3, 4, 7, 9, 11, 15, 16, 18)